Quotable
Quotes

THE GARDENER

Quotable Quotes

THE GARDENER

Magpie Books

LONDON

Constable & Robinson Ltd
3 The Lanchesters
162 Fulham Palace Road
London W6 9ER
www.constablerobinson.com

This edition published by Magpie Books,
an imprint of Constable & Robinson Ltd 2004

ISBN 1 84529 053 4

Compiled and designed by Tony and Penny Mills

A copy of the British Library Cataloguing in Publications Data
is available from the British Library

Printed and bound in the EU

Contents

Down The Garden Path

WHEN YOU LOOK AT a a person's garden, what is it like? Are there weeds everywhere, suggesting lazy upkeep? Is it unbearably neat and precise? Have they decided to grow their own vegetables? A garden can give away a lot about someone's secret habits.

When I go into my garden with a spade, and dig a bed, I feel such an exhilaration and health that I discover that I have been defrauding myself all this time in letting others do for me what I should have done with my own hands.

A Lecture Read before
the Mechanics Apprentices' Library Association
RALPH WALDO EMERSON
(1803–82)

Here at the fountains' sliding foot,
Or at some fruit-trees' mossy root,
Casting the body's vest aside,
My soul into the boughs does glide,
There like a bird, it sits and sings,
Then whets and combs its silver wings,
And, till prepared for longer flight,
Waves in its plumes the various light.

From *Thoughts in a Garden*
ANDREW MARVELL
(1621–78)

Thy plants are an orchard of pomegranates, with pleasant fruits; camphire, with spikenard, Spikenard and saffron; calamus and cinnamon, with all trees of frankincense: myrrh and aloes, with all the chief spices:

Awake, O north wind; and come, thou south; blow upon my garden, that the spices thereof may flow out. Let my beloved come into his garden, and eat his pleasant fruits.

The Song of Solomon, from The Bible

I see the beds of larkspur with purple eyes; tall hollyhocks, red or yellow; the broad sunflowers, caked in gold, with bees buzzing round them; wildernesses of pinks, and hot glowing peonies; poppies run to seed; the sugared lily, and faint mignonette, all ranged in order, and as thick as they can grow; the box-tree borders, the gravel-walks, the painted alcove, the confectionery, the clotted cream: – I think I see them now … All that I have observed since, of flowers and plants, and grass-plots, and of suburb delights, seems to me borrowed from 'that first garden of my innocence' – to be slips and scions stolen from that bed of memory.

Table-Talk Essays on Men and Manners
WILLIAM HAZLITT
(1778–1830)

I have a garden of my own
But so with roses overgrown
And lillies, that you would it guess
To be a little wilderness.

ANDREW MARVELL
(1621–78)

Ev'n in the stifling bosom of the town,
A garden, in which nothing thrives has charms
That soothes the rich possessor; much consol'd,
That here and there some sprigs of mournful
    mint,
Or nightshade, or valerian, grace the well
He cultivates.

From *The Task*
WILLIAM COWPER
(c.1664–1723)

By water to Fox-hall and there walked in Spring garden; a great deal of company, and the weather and garden pleasant; that it is very pleasant and cheap going thither, for a man may go to spend what he will, or nothing, all as one – but to hear the nightingale and other birds, and here fiddles, and there a harp, and here a jews trump, and here laughing, and there fine people walking, is mighty divertising. Among others, there were two pretty women alone, that walked a great while: which [being] discovered by some idle gentlemen, they would needs take them up; but to see the poor ladies, how they were put to it to run from them, and they after them: and sometimes the ladies put themselves along with other company, then the others drew back; at last, the ladies did get off out of the house and took boat and away.

Diary, 28th May 1667
SAMUEL PEPYS
(1633–1703)

And a country parson without some knowledge of plants is surely as incomplete as a country parsonage without a garden.

In a Gloucestershire Garden
CANON ELLACOMBE
1895

Adam walked by the rick-yard, at present empty of ricks to the little wooden gate leading into the garden … In that leafy, flowery, bushy time, to look for anyone in this garden was like playing at 'hide-and-seek'. There were the tall hollyhocks beginning to flower, and dazzle the eye with their pink, white and yellow; there were the syringas and Gueldres rose, all large and disorderly for want of trimming; there were leafy walls of scarlet beans and late peas; there was a row of bushy filberts in one direction and in another a huge apple-tree making a barren circle under its low-spreading boughs.

Adam Bede
GEORGE ELIOT
(1819–80)

Little strips in front of roadside cottages have a simple and tender charm that one may look for in vain in gardens of greater pretension ... for where else can one see such Wall-flowers, Or Double Daisies, or White Rose bushes; such clustering masses of perennial Peas, or such well-kept flowery edgings of Pink, or Thrift, or London Pride?

Home and Garden
GERTRUDE JEKYLL
(1843–1932)

Is there under heaven a more glorious and refreshing object of the kind, than an impregnable [holly] Hedge ... which I can shew in my poor gardens at any time of the year, glit'ring with its arm'd and vernished leaves, the taller standards at orderly distances blushing with their natural coral.

Sylva, or A Discourse on Forest trees
JOHN EVELYN
(1620–1706)

This cabin, Mary, in my sight appears,
Built as it has been in our waning years,
A rest afforded to our weary feet,
Preliminary to the last retreat.

Inscription
For an Hermitage in the Author's Garden
WILLIAM COWPER
(1731–1800)

On a summer's evening, when the large watering-pot has been filled and emptied some fourteen times, and the old couple have quite exhausted themselves by trotting about, you will see them sitting happily together in the little summerhouse, enjoying the calm and peace of the twilight, and watching the shadows as they fall upon the garden, and gradually growing thicker and more sombre, obscure the tints of their gayest flowers – no bad emblem of the years that have silently rolled over their heads, deadening in their course the brightest hues of early hopes and feelings which have long since faded away. These are their only recreations, and they require no more.

Sketches by Boz
CHARLES DICKENS
(1812–70)

Soon they came to a pleasant garden, where among the fairest flowers stood the hive, covered with vines and overhung with blossoming trees. Glow-worms stood at the door to light them home, and as they passed in, the Fairy thought how charming it must be to dwell in such a lovely place. The floor of wax was pure and white as marble, while the walls were formed of golden honey-comb, and the air was fragrant with the breath of flowers.

Flower Fables
LOUISA MAY ALCOTT
(1832–88)

And whither doe they [great kings and officers of state] withdraw themselves from the troublesome affayres of their estate, being tyred with the hearing and judging of litigious Controversies? choked… with the close ayres of their sumptuous buildings, their stomacks cloyed with varietie of Banquets, their eares filled and over-burthened with tedious discoursings. Wither? but into their Orchards? made and prepared, dressed and destinated for that purpose to renew and refresh their sences, and to call home their over-wearied spirits. Nay, it is … a comfort to them, to set open their Cazements into a most delicate Garden and Orchard, whereby they may not only see that, wherein they are so much delighted, but also to give fresh, sweete, and pleasant ayre to their Galleries and Chambers.

A New Orchard and Garden
WILLIAM LAWSON
1618

If you saw my little back yard, 'Wot a pretty
    spot!' you'd cry —
    It's a picture on a sunny summer day;
Wiv the turnip-tops and cabbages wot people
    doesn't buy
    I makes it on a Sunday look so gay.
The neighbours fink I grows 'em and you'd fancy
    you're in Kent,
    Or at Epsom, if you gaze into the mews;
It's a wonder as the landlord doesn't want to
    raise the rent,
    Because we've got such nobbly distant views.

Chorus

Oh! it really is a werry pretty garden,
And Chingford to the eastward could be seen;
    Wiv a ladder and some glasses,
    You could see to 'Ackney Marshes,
If it wasn't for the 'ouses in between.

'The Cockney's Garden'
EDGAR BATEMAN
(19th Century)

I went for the first time in my life, some years ago, to stay at a very grand and beautiful place in the country, where the grounds are said to be laid out with consummate taste. For the first three or four days I was perfectly enchanted; it seemed something so much better than nature … In three days' time I was tired to death; a thistle, a nettle, a heap of dead bushes, anything that wore the appearance of accident and want of intention was quite a relief. I used to escape from the made grounds, and walk upon an adjacent goose-common, where the cart-ruts, gravel pits, bumps, irregularities, coarse ungentlemanlike grass, and all the varieties produced by neglect, were a thousand times more gratifying than the monotony of beauties the result of design, and crowded into narrow confines with a luxuriance and abundance utterly unknown to nature.

SYDNEY SMITH
(1774–1847)

These gardens of New College are indescribably beautiful – not gardens in our American sense, but lawns of the richest green and softest velvet grass, shadowed over by ancient trees that have lived a quiet life here for centuries, and have been nursed and tended with such care.

English Note Books (Oxford)
NATHANIEL HAWTHORNE
(1807–64)

I know a little garden close
Set thick with lily and red rose
Where I would wander if I might
From dewy dawn to dewy night,
And have one with me wandering.

WILLIAM MORRIS
(1834–96)

Here, free from riot's hated noise,
Be mine, ye calmer, purer joys,
   A book or friend bestows;
Far from the storms that shake the great,
Contentment's gale shall fan my seat,
   And sweeten my repose.

Inscription
For a Moss-House in the Shrubbery at Weston
WILLIAM COWPER
(1731–1800)

Had I a garden, it should lie
   All smiling in the sun,
And after bud and butterfly
   Children should romp and run;
Filling their little laps with flowers,
   The air with shout and song,
While golden-crests in guelder bowers
   Rippled the whole day long.

from *'The Garden that I love'*
ALFRED AUSTIN
(1835–1913)

What a transition for a countryman visiting London for the first time – the passing from the crowded Strand or Fleet Street, by unexpected avenues, into [the Temple's] magnificent ample squares, its classic green recesses! What a cheerful, liberal look hath that portion of it, which, from three sides, overlooks the greater garden; that goodly pile

CHARLES LAMB
(1775–1834)

The man who has planted a garden feels that he has done something for the good of the World. He belongs to the producers. It is a pleasure to eat of the fruit of one's toil, if it be nothing more than a head of lettuce or an ear of corn. One cultivates a lawn even with great satisfaction; for there is nothing more beautiful than grass and turf in our latitude. The tropics may have their delights, but they have not turf: and the world without turf is a dreary desert.

My Summer in a Garden
CHARLES DUDLEY WARNER
(1829–1900)

But there are sounds that haunt a garden hardly less delightful than its sights and scents. What sound has more poetry in it than when in the early morning one hears the strong sharp sweep of the scythe, as it whistles through the falling grass, or the shrill murmur of the blade upon the whetstone; and in spite of mowing machines, at times one hears the old sounds still.

A Year in a Lancashire Garden
HENRY A. BRIGHT
1901

What pleasure have not children in applying their little green watering-pans to plants in pots, or pouring water in at the roots of favourite flowers at borders? And what can be more rational than the satisfaction which the grownup amateur, or master of the house, enjoys, when he returns from the city to his garden in the summer evenings and applies a syringe to his wall trees, with refreshing enjoyment to himself and the plants, and to the delight of his children.

The Suburban Garden and Villa Companion
J.C. LOUDON
1838

There is not a sprig of grass that shoots uninteresting to me.

THOMAS JEFFERSON
(1743–1826)

The houses I love best are those where warm old red bricks and old roses seem to melt into each other; where open french windows invite me onto a spacious lawn; where a terrace or ha-ha seamlessly conceal the break between the garden and the field or park beyond and where old and leafy trees offer shade on a summer's day.

Distant Days
WILLIAM FITZROY
(1851–1924)

The peace and love of a contented family should be echoed in the happy conjunction of their garden plants; each member offering a different character, but each living harmoniously together.

Greensleeves Again
ALBERT SMITHSON
(1884–1940)

A garden wall without a climbing rose, or a well-trained peach, is as meaningless to a gardener as a blank canvas is to an artist

DANIEL FROGGETT, garden designer
1955

The pride of my heart and the delight of my eyes is my garden ... Fancy a small plot of ground, with a pretty low irregular cottage at one end; a large granary, divided from the dwelling by a little court running along one side; and a long thatched shed, open towards the garden and supported by wooden pillars, at the other ... The house, granary, wall and paling are covered with vines, cherry-trees, roses, honeysuckles, and jessamines, with great clusters of tall hollyhocks running up between them; a large elder overhanging a little gate, and a magnificent bay tree ... This is my garden.

Our Village
MARY RUSSELL MITFORD
(1787–1855)

26

How proudly he talks
Of zigzags and walks;
And all the day raves
Of cradles and caves;
And boasts of his feats,
His grottos and seats;
Shows all his gewgaws,
And gapes for applause!
A fine occupation
For one of his station!
A hole where a rabbit
Would scorn to inhabit,
Dug out in an hour
He calls it a bow'r.

From 'My Lady's Lamentation
and Complaint against the Dean'
JONATHAN SWIFT
(1667–1745)

Flowers

LIKE MUSIC, FLOWERS HAVE the power to speak directly to the heart and awaken old memories and dreams. A single rose on *St Valentine's Day*, a primrose in the hedgerow, apple blossom and michaelmas daisies — what happiness they can promise or recall!

That which we call a rose
By any other name would smell as sweet.

Romeo and Juliet
WILLIAM SHAKESPEARE
(1564–1616)

A nd why take ye thought for raiment?
Consider the lilies of the field, how they grow; they toil not, neither do they spin: And yet I say unto you, That even Solomon in all his glory was not arrayed like one of these. Wherefore, if God so clothe the grass of the field, which to day is, and to morrow is cast into the oven, shall he not much more clothe you, O ye of little faith?

Matthew
6: 28–30

O ne of the most attractive things about
the flowers is their beautiful reserve.

Journals, 1906
HENRY DAVID THOREAU
(1817–62)

Flowers are Love's truest language; they betray,
Like the divining rods of Marigold,
Where precious wealth lies buried, not of gold,
But love – strong love, that never can decay!

Sonnet
PARK BENJAMIN
(1809–64)

There is scarcely any Rose that we can wish to
have in our gardens that is not also delightful
in the cut state. A china bowl filled with well-
grown Hybrid Perpetuals, grand of colour and
sweetly scented, is a room decoration that can
hardly be beaten both for beauty and for the
pleasure it gives, whether in a sitting-room or on
the breakfast table. The only weak point about
cut Roses is that their life is short.

Roses for English Gardens
GERTRUDE JEKYLL
(1843–1932)

Enter then the rose garden when the first sunshine sparkles in the dew, and enjoy with thankful happiness one of the loveliest scenes on earth ... There are white roses, striped roses, crimson roses, scarlet roses, vermillion roses, maroon roses, purple roses, roses almost black, and roses of glowing gold! What diversity and yet what harmony of outline!

A Book About Roses
S. REYNOLDS HOLE
(1819–1904)

The red rose whispers of passion,
And the white rose breathes of love;
O, the red rose is a falcon,
And the white rose is a dove.
But I send you a cream-white rosebud
With a flush on its petal tips;
For the love that is purest and sweetest
Has a kiss of desire on the lips.

A White Rose
JOHN BOYLE O'REILLY
(1844–90)

We are slumberous poppies,
　　Lords of Lethe downs,
Some awake, and some asleep,
　　Sleeping in our crowns,
What perchance our dreams may know,
　　Let our serious beauty show.

Central depths of purple,
　　Leaves more bright than rose,
Who shall tell what brightest thought
　　Out of darkest grows?
Who, through what funereal pain,
　　Souls to love and peace attain?

Chorus and Songs of the Flowers
LEIGH HUNT
(1784—1859)

The Crowne-Emperiall is of all flowers both Forraigne and home-bred, the delicatest and strangest: it hath the true shape of an Emperiall Crowne, and will be of divers colours, according to the *Art of the Gardner*. In the middest of the flower you shall see a round Pearle stand, in proportion, colour, and orientnesie like a true naturall Pearle, only it is of a soft liquid substance.

Home and Garden
GERTRUDE JEKYLL
(1843–1932)

That [conserve] of Cowslips doth marvelously strengthen the Braine, preserveth agaainst Madnesse, against decay of memory, stopeth Head-ache and most infirmities thereof.

A Book of Fruit and Flowers
THOMAS JENNER
1653

If there were nothing else to trouble us, the fate of the flowers would make us sad.

Aphorisms and Reflections
JOHN LANCASTER SPALDING
(1840–1916)

Flowers through their beautie, variety of colour and exquisite forme doe bring to a liberall and gentlemanly minde, the remembrance of honestie, comelinesse and all kinds of vertues. For it would be an unseemly thing (as a certain wise man saith) for him that doth looke upon and handle faire and beautifull things, and who frequenteth and is conversant in faire and beautifull places to have his minde not faire but deformed.

The Herball
JOHN GERARD
(1545–1612)

'How can you all talk so nicely?' Alice said, hoping to get the Tiger-lily into a better temper by a compliment. 'I have been in many gardens before, but none of the flowers could talk.'

'Put your hand down, and feel the ground,' said the Tiger-lily. 'Then you'll know why.'

Alice did so. 'It's very hard,' she said, 'but I don't see what that has to do with it.'

'In most gardens,' the Tiger-lily said, 'they make the beds too soft — so the flowers are always asleep.'

Through the Looking Glass
LEWIS CARROLL
(1832–98)

Stately stand the sunflowers, glowing down the
    garden-side,
Ranged in royal rank, a row along the warm grey
    wall,
Whence their deep disks burn at rich midnoon
    afire with pride,
Even as though their beams indeed were
    sunbeams, and the tall
Sceptral stems bore stars whose reign endures,
    not flowers that fall.

'The Mill Garden'
ALGERNON CHARLES SWINBURNE
(1837–1909)

In the garden were to be seen the most
wonderful flowers, and to the costliest of them
silver bells were tied, which sounded, so that
nobody should pass by without noticing the
flowers.

Tales
HANS CHRISTIAN ANDERSEN
(1805–75)

Within my little garden is a flower,
A tuft of flowers most like a sheaf of corn,
The lilac-blossomed daisy that is born
At Michaelmas, wrought by the gentle power
Of this sweet autumn into one bright shower
Of bloomy beauty. Spring hath nought more fair.
Four sister butterflies inhabit there,
Gay gentle creatures! Round that odorous bower
They weave their dance of joy the livelong day,
Seeming to bless the sunshine; and at night
Fold their enamelled wings as if to pray.
Home-loving pretty ones! would that I might
For richer gifts as cheerful tribute pay,
So meet the rising dawn, so hail the parting ray.

MARY RUSSELL MITFORD
(1787–1855)

Plant your rose in a good square hole, keep it weeded; prune it once a year, thoroughly; apply a spade of manure in February and you will have blooms for the rest of your life.

Easy Days
MARGARET MILLFIELD
1931

After this he led them into his garden, where was great variety of flowers; and he said, do you see all these? So Christiana said, Yes. Then said he again, Behold the flowers are diverse in stature, in quality, and colour, and smell and virtue, and some are better than others; also, where the gardener hath set them, there they stand, and quarrel not with one another.

JOHN BUNYAN
(1628–88)

Whatever doubts may be entertained as to the practicability of a lady attending to the culture of culinary vegetables and fruit trees, none can exist respecting her management of the flower garden. That is pre-eminently a woman's department. The culture of flowers implies the lightest possible of garden labour.

Practical Instructions in Gardening for Ladies
JANE LOUDON
1840

S weet flowers are slow
and weeds make haste.

WILLIAM SHAKESPEARE
(1564–1616)

It is often amusing to trace a fashion as it percolates downwards. By the time it has reached the far-away sleepy villages something quite new and entirely opposite is really the rage among the upper ten thousand. Cottages now try to fill their little plots with geraniums and calceolarias, which they are obliged to keep indoors at great inconvenience to themselves and loss of light to their rooms.

Social Twitters
MRS LOFTIE
1879

'I say, old fellow', remarked to me a friend … 'those Rose-trees which you recommended me to get, turned out a regular do. Cost a hatful of money – precious near a tenner, if not all out – and, by Jove, Sir! our curate at the county flower-show came and licked them all into fits!'

'Robert', I responded (I was too indignant to address him with Bob, as usual), 'I never in my life recommended a person of your profound ignorance to have anything to do with roses. You asked me to give you a list of the best, and I did so reluctantly, knowing that you had neither the taste nor the energy to do them justice. As to the outlay, the animal on which you have recklessly placed yourself … cost you, I know, more than eighty guineas; and for a tithe of that sum, without further supervision or effort, you expect a beautiful Rose-garden. I rejoice to hear that the curate beat you.'

A Book about Roses
DEAN HOLE
1901

Pondering shadows, colors, clouds
Grass-buds, and caterpillar shrouds
Boughs on which the wild bees settle,
Tints that spot the violet's petal.

Woodnotes
RALPH WALDO EMERSON
(1803–82)

'Oh tiger-lily!' said Alice, addressing herself to one that was waving gracefully about in the wind, 'I wish you could talk!'

'We can talk,' said the Tiger-lily, 'when there's anybody worth talking to' ...

'And can all the flowers talk?'

'As well as you can,' said the Tiger-lily. 'And a great deal louder.'

'It isn't manners for us to begin, you know,' said the Rose.

Through the Looking Glass
LEWIS CARROLL
(1832–98)

One is never thoroughly sociable with flowers till they are naturised, as it were christened, provided with decent, homely, well-wearing English names.

Our Village
MARY RUSSELL MITFORD
(1787–1855)

Daisy roots ... be good to keep up and strengthen the edges of your borders, as Pinks, be they red white, mixt.

The Country Housewife's Garden
WILLIAM LAWSON
1615

RECIPE FOR HONEY OF VIOLETS

Take of the Flowers of Vyolets 1 parte, of good Honey, 111 partes, seeth them with a softe fier.

Bulwarke of Defence etc
BULLEIN
1562

That straine again! It had a dying fall:
O it cam o'er my ear like the sweet sound
That breathes upon a bank of Violets,
Stealing and giving odour.

Twelfth Night
WILLIAM SHAKESPEARE
(1564–1616)

I hope you have a good store of double violets –
I think they are the Princesses of flowers, and
in a shower of rain almost as fine as barley sugar
drops are to a schoolboy's tongue.

Letter to Fanny Keats
JOHN KEATS
(1795–1821)

The chrysanthemem more almost than any other flower suffers from that megalomania which is the British gardener's sole idea of beauty. All he cares for is to get a thing large; farewell colour, fragrance, elegance, so long as you have a vast draggled head that looks like a moulting mop dipped in stale lobster sauce.

My Rock Garden
REGINALD FARRAR
(1880–1920)

How fresh, O Lord, how sweet and clean
Are thy returns! ev'nst as the flowers in spring:
   To which, besides their own demean,
The late-past frosts tributes of pleasure bring.
      Grief melts away
      Like snow in May
As if there were no such cold thing.

From 'The Flower'
GEORGE HERBERT
(1593–1633)

Flower in the crannied wall,
I pluck you out of the crannies:—
Hold you here, root and all, in my hand.
Little flower— but if I could understand
What you are, root and all, and all in all
I should know what God and man is.

ALFRED, LORD TENNYSON
(1809–92)

Flowers out of season, trouble
without reason.

OLD SAYING

Mrs Masters's fuschias's hung
Higher and broader, and brightly swung,
   Belllike, more and more
Over the narrow garden-path,
Giving the passe a sprinkle-bath
      In the morning.

She put up with their pushful ways,
And made us tenderly lift their sprays,
   Going to her door:
But when her funeral had to pass
They cut back all the flowery mass
      In the morning.

'The Lodgin-House Fuschias'
THOMAS HARDY
(1840–1928)

Flowers seem intended for the
solace of ordinary humanity ...
They are the cottager's treasure.

JOHN RUSKIN
(1819–1900)

Digging and Delving

*W*ITH WHAT PLEASURE *we look at our spade and fork and hoe in the morning; how well these old garden tools fit our hands; our fathers a thousand years ago would feel at home with them; true and honest, they have stood the test of time. In the evening, when with blistered hands and aching back we return them to their places, our thoughts may be less nostalgic (even much less printable).*

The good gardener knows with absolute certainty that if he does his part, if he gives the labour, the love, and every aid that his knowledge of his craft, experience of the conditions of his place, and exercise of his personal wit can work together to suggest, that so surely will God give the increase. Then with the honestly-earned success comes the consciousness of encouragement to renewed effort, and, as it were, an echo of the gracious words, 'Well done, good and faithful servant.'

Wood and Garden
GERTRUDE JEKYLL
(1843–1932)

Gardening requires lots of water – most of it in the form of perspiration.

Atlanta Journal and Constitution
LOU ERICKSON
(1840–1921)

Man was not made to rust out in idleness. A degree of exercise is as necessary for the preservation of health, both of body and mind, as his daily food. And what exercise is more fitting, or more appropriate of one who is in the decline of life, than that of superintending a well-ordered garden? What more enlivens the sinking mind? What is more conducive to a long life?

JOSEPH BRECK
(1794–1873)

CICELY: When I see a spade, I call it a spade.

GWENDOLEN: I am glad to say that I have never seen a spade. It is obvious that our social spheres have been widely different.

The Importance of Being Earnest
OSCAR WILDE
(1854–1900)

To pour water, therefore, upon plants, or upon the ground where they are growing, or where seeds are sown, is never of much use, and is generally mischievous; for, the air is dry; the sun comes immediately and bakes the ground, and vegetation is checked, rather than advanced, by the Operation. The best protector against frequent drought is frequent *digging*; or, in the fields, *ploughing*, and always *deep*. Hence will arise a *fermentation* and *dews*.

The English Gardener
WILLIAM COBBETT
(1762–1835)

Come, my spade. There is no ancient gentleman gardeners, ditchers and gravemakers; they hold up Adam's profession.

Hamlet
WILLIAM SHAKESPEARE
(1564–1616)

That such gardens are a real pleasure and refreshment to the owners we all know, and they are none the less so when the refreshment is taken in hard manual labour, for many a country parson can bear witness that 'the very works of and in an orchard and garden are better than the ease and rest of and from other labores.'

In a Gloucestershire Garden
CANON ELLACOMBE
1895

To dig in the mellow soil – to dig moderately, for all pleasure should be taken sparingly – is a great thing. One gets strength out of the ground as often as one really touches it with a hoe.

My Summer in a Garden
CHARLES DUDLEY WARNER
(1829–1900)

The gardener's work is never at an end; it begins with the year, and continues to the next: he prepares the ground, and then he sows it; after that he plants, and then he gathers the fruits.

Kalendarium Hortensis
JOHN EVELYN
(1620–1706)

Weeds Never Die.

DANISH PROVERB

Paid a labourer in the garden one day, 1s. 3d. How I wish I had once more the strength of my youth.

Diary, 13th April 1760
WILLIAM MARLOWE

It is quite useless, indeed it is grossly absurd, to prepare land and to incur trouble and expense, without duly, and even *very carefully*, attending to the *seed* that we are going to sow. The *sort*, the *genuineness*, the *soundness*, are all matters to be attended to, if we mean to avoid mortification and loss.

The English Gardener
WILLIAM COBBETT
(1762–1835)

When Adam dug and Eve span,
Who was then the gentleman?

OLD SAYING

I've often heard people cite old Adam as an example of the diligent gardener; but living in the Garden of Eden, with the richest soil in the world and God as his landscape designer, he had an unfair start

HAL SPEED, Contemporary Garden Designer
(1998)

Why are husbands like lawn mowers?
They are difficult to get started, emit foul smells, and don't work half the time.

AUTHOR UNKNOWN

He that would perfect his work must first sharpen his tools.

CONFUCIUS
(551–479 BC)

Reader, did you ever see a tender mother soothe a child to sleep, and afterwards lay it down to rest? ... an experienced eye can tell whether a proper degree of repose (so to speak) is given to a plant when committed to the earth, and from the way in which this is done, can predict the future destiny of the shrub or tree.

The Amateur Gardener's Year-Book
REV. HENRY BURGESS
1854

A lady, with a small light spade may, by repeatedly digging over the same line, and taking out only a little earth at a time, succeed in doing all the digging that can be required in a small garden; and she will not only have the satisfaction of seeing the garden created, as it were, by her own hands, but she will find her health and spirits wonderfully improved by the exercise, and by the reviving smell of the fresh earth.

Gardening for Ladies
JANE LOUDON
1840

A weed is but an unloved flower.

ELLA WHEELER WILCOX
(1850–1919)

A ring around the moon or sun,
and rain approaches on the run.

OLD SAYING

There is a lovable quality about the actual tools. One feels so kindly to the thing that enables the hand to obey the brain. Moreover, one feels a good deal of respect for it; without it the brain and the hand would be helpless.

GERTRUDE JEKYLL
(1843–1932)

The love of dirt is among the earliest of passions, as it is the latest. Mud-pies gratify one of our first and best instincts. Broad acres are a patent of nobility; and no man but feels more, of a man in the world if he have a bit of ground that he can call his own. However small it is on the surface, it is four thousand miles deep; and that is a very handsome property.

My Summer in a Garden
CHARLES DUDLEY WARNER
(1829–1900)

Spade! with which Wilkinson hath tilled
    his lands,
And shaped these pleasant walks by
    Emont's side,
Thou art a tool of honor in my hands,
I press thee, through a yielding soil,
    with pride.

WILLIAM WORDSWORTH
(1770–1850)

Tender-handed stroke a nettle
And it stings you for your pains;
Grasp it like a man of mettle,
And it soft as silk remains.

AARON HILL
(1685–1750)

M en have become the tools of
their tools.

HENRY DAVID THOREAU
(1817–62)

Doctor Pinck, later ward of New College in Oxon ... was a very learned man, and well versed in Physick, and truly he would rise very betimes in the morning, even in his later dayes, when he was almost four score years old, and going into his Garden he would take a Mattock or Spade, digging there an houre or two which he found very advanatgeous to his health ...

And if Gentlemen which have little else to doe, would be ruled by me, I would advise them to spend their spare time in their Gardens; either in digging, setting, weeding, or the like, than

which there is no better way in the world to preserve health. If a man want an Appetite to his Victuals, the smell of the Earth new turned up, by digging with a Spade will procure it and if he be inclined to a Consumption it will recover him.

Art of Simpling
WILLIAM COLES
1656

Il faut cultiver notre jardin.
We must cultivate
our own garden.

Candide
VOLTAIRE
(1694–1778)

M y good hoe as it bites the ground revenges my wrongs, and I have less lust to bite my enemies. In the smoothing of the rough hillocks, I smooth my temper.

RALPH WALDO EMERSON
(1803–82)

Mackerel sky,
rain is nigh.

OLD SAYING

Naturam expelles furca, tamen usque recurret.

You can drive out nature with a fork;
but she will always swiftly return.

HORACE
(65 BC–8 AD)

No occupation is so delightful to me as the culture of the earth and no culture comparable to that of the garden. Such a variety of subjects, some one always coming to perfection, the failure of one thing repaired by the success of another, and instead of one harvest a continued one through the year. Under a total of want of demand except for our family table, I am still devoted to the garden. But though an old man, I am but a young gardener.

Letter to Charles Willson Peale
THOMAS JEFFERSON
(1743–1826)

On no other ground
Can I sow my seed
Without tearing up
Some stinking weed.

WILLIAM BLAKE
(1757–1827)

Tickle it with a hoe and it will
laugh into a harvest.

ENGLISH SAYING

Hoeing in the garden on a bright, soft May
day, when you are not obliged to, is nearly
equal to the delight of going trouting.

My Summer in a Garden
CHARLES DUDLEY WARNER
(1829–1900)

The Gardener does not love to talk
He makes me keep the gravel walk;
And when he puts his tools away,
He locks the door and takes the key.

Away behind the currant row
Where no one else but Cook may go,
Far in the plots, I see him dig
Old and serious, brown and big.

He digs the flowers, green, red and blue,
Nor wishes to be spoken to.
He digs the flowers and cuts the haym
And never seems to want to play.

Silly gardener! summer goes,
And winter comes with pinching toes,
When in the garden bare and brown
You must lay your barrow down.

Well now, and while the summer stays
To profit by these garden days
O how much wiser you would be
To play at Indian wars with me!

The Gardener
ROBERT LOUIS STEVENSEN
(1850–94)

The great reward of digging is the promise of
next year's harvest. A well dug trench is
worth as much as a guinea in the bank.

SAMUEL MAXWELL
1912

The man who undertakes a garden is relentlessly pursued. He felicitates himself that, when he gets it once planted, he will have a season of rest and of enjoyment in the sprouting and growing of his seeds. It is a green anticipation. He has planted a seed that will keep him awake nights; drive rest from his bones, and sleep from his pillow. Hardly is the garden planted, when he must begin to hoe it.

My Summer in a Garden
CHARLES DUDLEY WARNER
(1829–1900)

Through cunning with dibble, rake, mattock,
    and spade,
By line and by level, trim garden is made.

Five Hundred Points of Good Husbandry
THOMAS TUSSER
(C.1520–80)

Oh how I've tugged and pulled at the twisted roots of nettles in my wild garden, following the stringy yellow fibres a yard or more along the ground; or worse still have been my struggles with 'ground elder', which made its way everywhere. It was a yearly toil, but at last I conquered, and made the weeds understand that although wild, yet it was a flower and not a 'bear garden'.

Children's Gardens
THE HON. MRS EVELYN CECIL
1907

Never perform any operation without gloves on your hands that you can do with gloves on; even weeding is far more effectually and expeditiously performed by gloves... Thus, no gardener need have hands like bears' paws.

J.C. LOUDON
The Villa Gardener
1850

The best [garden rollers] are made of the hardest marble ... procured from the ruins of many places in Smyrna when old columns of demolished antiquities are being sawed off ... [they] may be procured by the friendship of some merchant trading into the Levant.

Elysium Britannicum
JOHN EVELYN
1659

There will ever be something to do. Weeds are always growing; the great Mother of all living creatures is full of seed in her bowels, and any stirring gives them heat of sun, and being laid near day, they grow.

A New Orchard and Garden
WILLIAM LAWSON
1618

One year's seed, seven years weed.

OLD SAYING

Agriculture is still at a very barbarous stage. I hope to live to see the day when I can do my gardening, as tragedy is done, to slow and soothing music ... I almost expect to find a cooling drink and hospitable entertainment at the end of a row. But I never do. There is nothing to be done but to hoe back to the other end.

My Summer in a Garden
CHARLES DUDLEY WARNER
(1829–1900)

Though the Camomile the more it is trodden on the faster it grow, yet youth the more it is wasted the sooner it wears.

From *Henry IV Part I*
WILLIAM SHAKESPEARE
(1564–1616)

... the gardener
Should with rich mould or asses' solid dung
    Or other ordure glut the starving earth
Bearing full baskets straining with the weight,
    Nor should he hesitate to bring as food
For new-ploughed fallow-ground whatever stuff
    The privy vomits from its filthy sewers.

De Re Rustica
COLUMELLA
(1st century)

There were in ancient time, as Pliny record-
eth, certaine wittie husbandmen, that wholly
refused and forbad the dunging of Gardens placed
nigh to the dwelling houses: in that this dunging
might infect the aire thereabout.

The Gardener's Labyrinth
THOMAS HILL
1577

I know ladies who love gardening, and have a limited number of favourites which they tend with their own fair hands, but are often at fault in reference to the soil which they should employ for potting ... Night soil and pigeon-dung and sugar baker's scum are rather ill-favoured materials to have to manipulate ... good turfy loam from an old mead is the ne plus ultra; its value cannot be too highly estimated.

The Amateur Gardener's Year-Book
REV HENRY BERGESS
1854

The Seasons

*T*HE PATIENT AND *philosophical gardener welcomes the mixture of reward and challenge that each season offers; the lazy and impatient fumes at the watering in summer and the digging in winter. What type are you?*

By the 14th of January the snow was entirely gone; the turnips emerged not damaged at all, save in sunny places; the wheat looked delicately, and the garden plants were well preserved; for snow is the most kindly mantle that infant vegetation can be wrapped in; were it not for that friendly meteor no vegetable life could exist at all in northerly regions.

The Natural History of Selborne
GILBERT WHITE
(1720–93)

March comes in with an Adder's head
And goes out with a Peacock's tail.

OLD SAYING

Cut all thing or gather the Moone in the wane,
But soe in encreasing, or give it his bane.
[Harvest when the moon is waning, plant when it is waxing, or face the consequences.]

Five Hundred Points of Good Husbandry
THOMAS TUSSER
(C.1520–80)

For winter's rains and ruins are over,
And all the seasons of snows and sins;
The days dividing lover and lover,
The light that loses, the night that wins;
And time remembered is grief forgotten,
And frosts are slain and flowers begotten,
And in green underwood and cover
Blossom by blossom the spring begins.

ALGERNON CHARLES SWINBURNE
(1837–1909)

The year's at the spring,
And day's at the morn;
Morning's at seven;
The hill-side's dew-pearl'd;
The lark's on the wing;
The snail's on the thorn;
God's in His heaven –
All's right with the world!

'Pippa's Song'
ROBERT BROWNING
(1812–89)

Lo, the winter is past, the rain is over and gone; the flowers appear again upon the earth; the time of the singing of birds is come, and the voice of the turtle [dove] is heard in our land. The fig tree putteth forth her green figs, and the vines with the tender grape give a good smell. Arise, my love, my fair one, and come away.

The Song of Solomon, from the Bible

It was the beginning of April, when the primroses are in bloom, and a warm wind blows over the flower-beds newly turned, and the gardens, like women, seem to be getting ready for the summer fetes.

Madame Bovary
GUSTAVE FLAUBERT
(1821–80)

Now 'tis the spring, and weeds are shallow-
rooted;
Suffer them now, and they'll outgrow the
garden,
And choke the herbs for want of
husbandry.

Queen Margaret, in *Henry VI*
WILLIAM SHAKESPEARE
(1564–1616)

I do hope, that it is unnecessary for me to say,
that sowing according to the moon is wholly
absurd and ridiculous; and that it arose solely out
of the circumstance, that our forefathers, who
could not read, had neither almanack nor
calendar to guide them, and counted by moons
and festivals, instead of by months, and days of
months.

The English Gardener
WILLIAM COBBETT
(1762–1835)

See the land her Easter Keeping,
    Rises as her Maker rose.
Seeds, so long in darkness sleeping,
    Burst at last from winter snows.
Earth with heaven above rejoices;
    Fields and gardens hail the spring;
Shores and woodlands ring with voices,
    While the wild birds build and sing.

'Easter Week'
CHARLES KINGSLEY
(1819–75)

In March and in April, from morning to night,
In sowing and setting, good houswives delight:
To have in a garden, or other like plot,
To turn up their house and to furnish their pot.

Five Hundred Points of Good Husbandry
THOMAS TUSSER
(C.1520–80)

Just now the lilac is in bloom,
All before my little room;
And in my flower-beds, I think,
Smile the carnation and the pink;
And down the borders, well I know,
The poppy and the pansy blow.
Oh! there the chestnuts, summer through,
Beside the river make for you
A tunnel of green gloom, and sleep
Deeply above; and green and deep
The stream mysterious glides beneath,
Green as a dream and deep as death.

'The Old Vicarage, Grantchester'
RUPERT BROOKE
(1887–1915)

Spring's real glory dwells not in the meaning,
    Gracious though it be, of her blue hours;
But is hidden in her tender leaning
    To the Summer's richer wealth of flowers.

Dawn is fair because the mists fade slowly
    Into day, which floods the world with light:
Twilight's mystery is so sweet and holy,
Just because it ends in starry night.

ADELAIDE PROCTOR
(1811–57)

At spring (for the sommer) sowe garden ye shall,
    At harvest (for winter) or sowe not at all.
Oft digging, removing, and weeding (ye see),
    Make herbe the more holesome and greater
      to bee.
Time fair, to sowe or to gather be bold,
    But set or remoove when the weather is cold.

Five Hundred Points of Good Husbandry
THOMAS TUSSER
(C.1520–80)

Rain, do not hurt my flowers, but quickly spread
Your hony drops: presse not to smell them here:
When they are ripe, their odour will ascend
And at your lodging with their thanks appear.

GEORGE HERBERT
(1593–1633)

There is no time like the old time, when you and
    I were young,
When the buds of April blossomed, and the birds
    of spring-time sung!
The garden's brightest glories by summer suns
    are nursed,
But oh, the sweet, sweet violets, the flowers that
    opened first!

OLIVER WENDELL HOLMES
(1809–94)

Enjoy the spring, children, to the full, for it is indeed a lovely time, and like your own childhood, should be full of promise, and fresh, gay, happy innocence. But with new life comes new work ... and business must start in real earnest now. It is not only pretty trees and flowers that begin to grow, but the revival comes to weeds as well, and very soon they will choke and kill the more tender plants; so the first duty in spring is to weed.

THE HON. MRS EVELYN CECIL

Children's Gardens

1907

'O for the Thames, and its rippling reaches,
  Where almond rushes, and breezes sport!
Take me a walk under Burnham Beeches;
  Give me a dinner at Hampton Court!'
Poets, be still, though your hearts I harden;
  We've flowers by day and have scents at dark,
The limes are in leaf in the cockney garden,
  And lilacs blossom in Regent's Park.

From 'Rus In Urbe'
CLEMENT WILLIAM SCOTT
(b. 1841)

I know of nothing that makes one feel more complacent, in these July days, than to have his vegetables from his own garden.

My Summer in a Garden
CHARLES DUDLEY WARNER
(1829–1900)

Soon will the high Midsummer pomps come on,
Soon will the musk carnations break and swell,
Soon shall we have gold-dusted snap-dragon,
Sweet William with its homely cottage smell,
And stocks in fragrant blow;
Roses that down the alleys shine afar,
And open, jasmine-muffled lattices,
And groups under the dreaming garden-trees,
And the full moon and the white evening-star.

MATTHEW ARNOLD
(1822–88)

'Tis the last rose of summer,
Left blooming alone.

THOMAS MOORE
(1779–1852)

In these golden latter August days, Nature has come to a serene equilibrium. Having flowered and fruited, she is enjoying herself.

My Summer in a Garden
CHARLES DUDLEY WARNER
(1829–1900)

In fine weather the old gentleman is almost constantly in the garden; and when it is too wet to go into it, he will look out of the window at it, by the hour together. He has always something to do there, and you will see him digging, and sweeping, and cutting, and planting, with manifest delight. In spring-time, there is no end to the sowing of seeds, and sticking little bits of wood over them, with labels, which look like epitaphs to their memory; and in the evening, when the sun has gone down, the perseverance with which he lugs a great watering-pot about is perfectly astonishing ... The old lady is very fond of flowers, as the hyacinth-glasses in the parlour-window, and geranium-pots in the little front court, testify. She takes great pride in the garden too: and when one of the four fruit-trees produces rather a larger gooseberry than usual, it is carefully preserved under a wineglass on the sideboard, for the edification of visitors, who are duly informed that Mr. So-and-so planted the tree which produced it, with his own hands.

Sketches by Boz
CHARLES DICKENS
(1812–70)

Unloved, that beech will gather brown,
This maple burn itself away;
Unloved, the sun-flower, shining fair,
Ray round with flames her disk of seed,
And many a rose-carnation feed
With summer spice the humming air.

ALFRED TENNYSON
(1809–92)

Give me the splendid silent sun, with all his
    beams full-dazzling;
Give me juicy autumnal fruit, ripe and red from
    the orchard;
Give me a field where the unmow'd grass grows;
Give me an arbor, give me the trellis'd grape;
Give me fresh corn and wheat—give me serene-
    moving animals, teaching content.

'Leaves of Grass'
WALT WHITMAN
(1819–92)

In my Autumn garden I was fain
    To mourn among my scattered roses;
    Alas for that last rosebud that uncloses
To Autumn's languid sun and rain
When all the world is on the wane!
    Which has not felt the sweet constraint
      of June,
    Nor heard the nightingale in tune.

Broad-faced asters by my walk,
    You are but coarse compared with roses:
    More choice, more dear that rosebud which
        uncloses,
Faint-scented, pinched upon its stalk,
That least and last which cold winds balk;
    A rose it is though least and last of all,
    A rose to me though at the fall.

'An October Garden'
CHRINTINA ROSSETTI
(1830–94)

O Autumn, laden with fruit, and stained
With the blood of the grape, pass not, but sit
Beneath my shady roof; there thou mayst rest,
And tune thy jolly voice to my fresh pipe,
And all the daughters of the year shall dance!
Sing now the lusty song of fruits and flowers.

From 'To Autumn'
WILLIAM BLAKE
(1757–1827)

It is sometimes pleasant to make the earth yield her increase, and gather the fruits in their season; but the heroic spirit will not fail to dream of remoter retirements and more rugged paths. It will have its garden-plots and its parterres elsewhere than on the earth, and gather nuts and berries by the way for its subsistence, or orchard fruits with such heedlessness as berries.

HENRY DAVID THOREAU
(1817–62)

I like to go into the garden these warm latter days, and muse. To muse is to sit in the sun, and not think of anything ... This sitting in the sun amid the evidences of a ripe year is the

easiest part of gardening I have experienced. But
what a combat has gone on here! What vegetable
passions have run the whole gamut of ambition,
selfishness, greed of place, fruition, satiety, and
now rest here in the truce of exhaustion!

My Summer in a Garden
CHARLES DUDLEY WARNER
(1829–1900)

'The Spirits of the Air live on the smells
Of fruit; and Joy, with pinions light, roves round
The gardens, or sits singing in the trees.'
Thus sang the jolly Autumn as he sat;
Then rose, girded himself, and o'er the bleak
Hills fled from our sight: but left his golden load.

WILLIAM BLAKE
(1757–1827)

While conversing with the wife of a mechanic during the coldest period of the recent winter, she [a friend of the author's] observed that the parental bed seemed to be scantily and insufficiently clothed, and she inquired if there were no more blankets in the house. 'Yes, ma'am, we've another,' replied the housewife, 'but…' and here she paused. 'But what?', said the lady. 'It is not at home, ma'am.' 'Surely, surely it's not in pawn?' 'Oh dear no, ma'am; Tom has only just took it – just took it –' 'Well, Bessie, took it where?' 'Please, ma'am, he took it – took it – took it to keep the frost out of the greenhouse; and please, ma'am, we don't want it, and we're quite hot in bed.'

About Roses
DEAN HOLE
1901

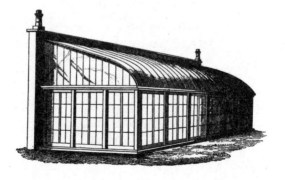

'There was a frost
Last night!' she said,
'And the stove we forgot
When we went to bed,
And the greenhouse plants
Are frozen dead!'
By the breakfast blaze
Blank-faced spoke she
Her scared young look
Seeming to be
The very symbol
Of tragedy.

The frost is fiercer
Than then to-day,
As I pass the place
Of her once dismay.
But the greenhouse stands
Warm, tight, and gay,

While she who grieved
At the sad lot
Of her pretty plants –
Cold, iced, forgot–
Herself is colder,
And knows it not.

The Frozen Greenhouse
THOMAS HARDY
(1840–1928)

In these golden October days no work is more fascinating than this getting ready for spring. The sun is no longer a burning enemy, but a friend, illuminating all the open space, and warming the mellow soil. And the pruning and clearing away of rubbish, and the fertilizing, go on with something of the hilarity of a wake, rather than the despondency of other funerals.

My Summer in a Garden
CHARLES DUDLEY WARNER
(1829–1900)

The seasons alter: hoary-headed frosts
Fall in the fresh lap of the crimson rose.

A Midsummer Night's Dream
WILLIAM SHAKESPEARE
(1564–1616)

Polly is picking up chestnuts on the sward, regardless of the high wind which rattles them about her head and upon the glass roof of her winter-garden. The garden, I see, is filled with thrifty plants, which will make it always summer there. The callas about the fountain will be in flower by Christmas: the plant appears to keep that holiday in her secret heart all summer.

My Summer in a Garden
CHARLES DUDLEY WARNER
(1829–1900)

Who loves a garden loves a greenhouse too.

The Task
WILLIAM COWPER
(1731–1800)

Winter is the time I put my feet up with a clear conscience; no weeds are growing; the hedges are trimmed; the lawn needs no work until the spring.

SIMON MILLS
1953

Oh the joys of opening the seed catalogues as they pop through my letter-box in late autumn and afford nightly reading and rereading until the new year. There are the biggest and tastiest vegetables you have ever seen; the most perfect flowers; the fruit cage, filled with bushes in neat and tidy rows. Oh, how perfect my garden will be next year, or, at worst, the year after, or when I retire…

MARTIN SANDYS
2001

Winter is the gardener's off-season. During the summer, football managers have the transfer window; we gardeners have the seed catalogue.

Dominic Finch
1999

I like a man who shaves (next to one who doesn't shave) to satisfy his own conscience, and not for display, and who dresses as neatly at home as he does anywhere. Such a man will be likely to put his garden in complete order before the snow comes, so that its last days shall not present a scene of melancholy ruin and decay.

My Summer in a Garden
Charles Dudley Warner
(1829–1900)

The Kitchen Garden

*T*HERE ARE FEW GREATER pleasures than picking peas straight from the pod to chew as you walk round your garden, and a new potato freshly dug is quite another species from anything brought home in cellophane from the supermarket. Munch on!

sure in a flower-garden, I have in a
en too, and for the same reason.
of cabbage-plants, or of peas or
...ng up, I immediately think of those
which I used so carefully to water of an evening
at Wem, when my day's tasks were done, and of
the pain with which I saw them droop and hang
down their leaves in the morning's sun.

Table-Talk Essays on Men and Manners
WILLIAM HAZLITT
(1778–1830)

When I pick a twig of Bay, or brush against a
bush of Rosemary, or tread upon a tuft of
Thyme, or pass through incense-laden brakes of
Cistus, I feel that here is all that is best and
purest and most refined, and nearest to poetry,
in the range of faculty of the sense of smell.

Home and Garden
GERTRUDE JEKYLL
(1843–1932)

Let husky wheat the haughs adorn,
An' aits set up their awnie horn,
An' pease and beans, at e'en or morn,
　　Perfume the plain:
Leeze me on thee, John Barleycorn,
　　Thou king o' grain!

Poems and Songs
ROBERT BURNS
(1759–96)

As to the produce of a garden, every middle-aged person of observation may perceive, within his own memory, both in town and country, how vastly the consumption of vegetables is increased. Green-stalls in cities now support multitudes in a comfortable state, while gardeners get fortunes. Every decent labourer also has his garden, which is half his support, as well as his delight; and common farmers provide plenty of beans, peas, and greens, for their hinds to eat with their bacon; and those few that do not are despised for their sordid parsimony.

The Natural History of Selborne
GILBERT WHITE
(1720–93)

Training is everything. The peach was once a bitter almond; cauliflower is nothing but cabbage with a college education.

MARK TWAIN
(1835–1910)

Daily the beans saw me come to their rescue armed with a hoe, and thin the ranks of their enemies, filling up the trenches with weed dead. May a lusty crest-waving Hector, that towered a whole foot above his crowding comrades, fell before my weapon and rolled in the dust.

HENRY DAVID THOREAU
(1817–62)

When the goose honks high,
Fair weather is nigh.

OLD SAYING

M r. Missing, a barrister, living in the parish of Titchfield, in Hampshire, and who was a most excellent and kind neighbour of mine, has a border under a south wall, on which he, and his father before him, have grown *early peas,* every year, for *more, now, than fifty years;* and if, at any time, they had been finer than they were every one year of the four or five years that I saw them, they must have been something very extraordinary; for, in those ears they were as fine and full bearing, as any that I ever saw in England.

The English Gardener
WILLIAM COBBETT
(1762–1835)

A little croft we owned – a plot of corn,
A garden stored with peas, and mint, and
    thyme,
And flowers for posies, oft on Sunday morn

Plucked while the church bells rang their
    earliest chime.
Can I forget our freaks at shearing time!
My hen's rich nest through long grass scarce
    espied;
The cowslip-gathering in June's dewy prime;
The swans that with white chests upreared in
    pride
Rushing and racing came to meet me at the
    water-side.

'Incidents Upon Salisbury Plain'
WILLIAM WORDSWORTH
(1770–1850)

It is not enough for a gardener to love his flowers and his vegetables; he must also hate weeds.

ANON.

The garden was one of those old-fashioned paradises which hardly exist any longer except as memories of our childhood. No finical separation between flower and kitchen garden there; no monotony of enjoyment for one sense to the exclusion of another; but a charming paradisiacal mingling of all that was pleasant to the eyes and good for food. The rich flower border running along every walk, with its endless succession of spring flowers, anemones, auriculas, wall-flowers, sweet williams, campanulas, snap-dragons, and tiger-lilies, had its taller beauties, such as moss and Provence roses, varied with espalier apple-trees; the crimson of a carnation was carried out in the lurking of the neighbouring strawberry-beds. You gathered a moss-rose one moment, and a bunch of currants the next; you were in a delicious fluctuation between the scent of jasmine and the juice of gooseberries.

GEORGE ELIOT
(1819–90)

Potatoes have prevailed in this little district, by means of premiums, within these twenty years only; and are much esteemed here now by the poor, who would scarce have ventured to taste them in the last reign.

The Natural History of Selborne
GILBERT WHITE
(1720–93)

Kale, there really seams to be very little reason for troubling one's self with this very course vegetable; for it is ridiculous to seek a variety in getting bad things to take their turn with good.

The English Gardener
WILLIAM COBBETT
(1762–1835)

... Let first the onion flourish there,
Rose among roots, the maiden-fair;
Let thyme the mountaineer (to dress)
The tinier birds and wading cress,
The lover of the shallow brook,
From all my plots and borders look.
Nor crisp and ruddy radish, nor
Pease-cods for the child's pinafore
Be lacking; nor of salad clan

The last and least that ever ran
About great nature's garden-beds.
Nor thence be missed the speary heads
Of artichoke; nor thence the bean
That gathered innocent and green
Outsavours the belauded pea.
These tend, I prithee ...
And I, being provided thus,
Shall, with superb asparagus,
A book, a taper, and a cup
Of country wine, divinely sup.

A Child's Garden of Verses and Underwoods
ROBERT LOUIS STEVENSON
(1850–94)

I hate the runner bean; I hate the humble pea;
I hate celery and radish and common salsify;
I hate the brussel sprout and foreign artichoke
I tremble and I shudder, it's lucky I don't croak.

'A List of Hates'
ADAM SHAW, Schoolboy, aged 12
2001

Whereas on summer days I see
That sacred herb, the Rosemary,
The which since once our Lady threw
Upon its flowers her robe of blue,
Has never shewn them white again,
But still in blue doth dress them —
Then, oh! then,
I think upon old friends and bless them.

Punch
1916

On fine days she went down into the garden. The dew had left on the cabbages a silver lace with long transparent threads spreading from one to the other. No birds were to be heard; everything seemed asleep, the espalier covered with straw, and the vine, like a great sick serpent under the coping of the wall, along which, on drawing near, one saw the many-footed woodlice crawling. Under the spruce by the hedgerow, the [statue of the] curé in the three-cornered hat reading his breviary had lost his right foot, and the very plaster, scaling off with the frost, had left white scars on his face.

Madame Bovary
GUSTAVE FLAUBERT
(1821–80)

For you there's rosemary and rue; these keep
Seeming and savour all the winter long.

The Winter's Tale
WILLIAM SHAKESPEARE
(1564–1616)

In summer cut a bough of bay
Eat rich stew 'til Easter Day.

COUNTRY SAYING

Where the parsley stays green all
year round, the wife wears the
trousers.

OLD SAYING

I plant rosemary all over the garden, so pleasant
is it to know that at every few steps one may
draw the kindly branchlets through one's hand,
and have the enjoyment of their incomparable
incense; and I grow it against walls, so that the
sun may draw out its inexhaustible sweetness to
greet me as I pass.

Home and Garden
GERTRUDE JEKYLL
(1843–1932)

The lettuce is to me a most interesting study. Lettuce is like conversation; it must be fresh and crisp, so sparkling that you scarecly notice the bitter of it. Lettuce, like most talkers, is, however, apt to run rapidly to seed.

My Summer in a Garden
CHARLES DUDLEY WARNER
(1829–1900)

Everyone knows the use of this excellent plant [spinach]. Pigs, who are excellent judges of the relative qualities of vegetables, will leave cabbages for lettuces, and lettuces for spinach.

The English Gardener
WILLIAM COBBETT
(1762–1835)

Fine bazell sowe, in a pot to growe
Fine seedes sowe now,
Before ye sawe how.
Fine bazell desireth it may be her lot,
To growe as the gilloflower, trim in a pot,
That ladies and gentils, for whom she doth serve,
May helpe hir as needeth, poor life to preserve.

THOMAS TUSSER
(c.1520–80)

As for recreation, if a man be weary with
over-much study (for study is a weariness to
the Flesh as Solomon can tell you) there is no
better place in the world to recreate himself than
a Garden, there being no sense but may be

110

delighted therein. If his sight be obfuscated and dull, with continual poring, there is no better way to relieve it than to view the pleasant green-esse of Herbes.

Art of Simpling
WILLIAM COLES
1656

Plant garlic on the shortest day,
harvest on the longest.

OLD SAYING

A ll who have gardens should fight against the deterioration of some of our best vegetables through the mania for size. Although the flavour of vegetables may not be so obvious as of fruit, it is often their essential quality ... Bad, too, is the raising of new varieties and abolishing old kinds from supposed deficiencies in size.

The Vegetable Garden
WILLIAM ROBINSON
1905

I led the way into the kitchen-garden. It was in the first promise of a summer profuse in vegetables and fruits. Perhaps it was not so much cared for as other parts of the property; but it was more attended to than most kitchen-gardens belonging to farm-houses. There were borders of flowers along each side of the gravel walks; and there was an old sheltering wail on the north side covered with tolerably choice fruit-trees; there was a slope down to the fish-pond at the end, where there were great strawberry-beds; and raspberry-bushes and rose-bushes grew wherever there was a space; it seemed a chance which had been planted. Long rows of peas stretched at right angles from the main walk, and I saw Phillis stooping down among them.

Cousin Phillis
ELIZABETH GASKELL
(1810–65)

Eat no onions nor garlic, for we are to utter sweet breath.

A Midsummer Night's Dream
WILLIAM SHAKESPEARE
(1564–1616)

Parsley before it is born is seen by the devil nine times.

OLD SAYING

There's never a garden in all the parish but what there's endless waste in it for want o' somebody as could use everything up. It's what I think to myself sometimes, as there need nobody run short of victuals if the land was made the most of. There was never a morsel but what could find its way to a mouth. It sets one thinking that – gardening does.

Silas Marner
GEORGE ELIOT
(1819–90)

Plant melons, harvest melons;
plant beans, harvest beans.
[ie, as ye sow, so shall ye reap]

PROVERB

Rue in thyme
should be a maiden's posie.

PROVERB

Turnips like a dry bed but a wet head.

OLD SAYING

He could walk, or rather turn about in his little garden, and feel more solid happiness from the flourishing of a cabbage or the growing of a turnip than was ever received from the most ostentatious show the vanity of man could possibly invent. He could delight himself with thinking, 'Here will I set such a root, because my Camilla likes it; here, such another, because it is my little David's favorite.'

The Adventures of David Simple
SARAH FIELDING
(1710–68)

My garden is run wild!
Where shall I plant anew –
For my bed, that once was covered
     with thyme,
Is all overrun with rue?

'The Seeds of Love'
MRS FLEETWOOD HABERGHAM
(d. 1703)

The man who picks peas steadily for a living is more than respectable, he is even envied by his shop-worn neighbors. We are as happy as the birds when our Good Genius permits us to pursue any outdoor work, without a sense of dissipation.

HENRY DAVID THOREAU
(1817–62)

I left my garden for a week, just at the close of the dry spell. A season of rain immediately set in, and when I returned the transformation was wonderful. In one week every vegetable had fairly jumped forward. The tomatoes which I left slender plants, eaten of bugs and debating whether they would go backward or forward, had become stout and lusty, with thick stems and dark leaves, and some of them had blossomed.

The most remarkable growth was the asparagus. There was not a spear above ground when I went away; and now it had sprung up, and gone to seed, and there were stalks higher than my head. I am entirely aware of the value of words, and of moral obligations. When I say that the asparagus had grown six feet in seven days, I expect and wish to be believed. I am a little particular about the statement; for, if there is any prize offered for asparagus at the next agricultural fair, I wish to compete.

My Summer in a Garden
CHARLES DUDLEY WARNER
(1829–1900)

As for Rosemarine [rosemary] I lett it runne all over my garden walls, not onlie because my bees love it, but because it is the herb sacred to remembrance and, therefore, to friendship; whence a sprig of it hath a dumb language that maketh it the chosen emblem of our funeral wakes and in our buriall grounds.

Sir Thomas More
(1478–1535)

In the knowledge of simples, wherein the manifold wisdom of God is wondeffully to be seen, one thing would be carefully observed – which is, to know what herbs may be used instead of drugs of the same nature, and to make the garden the shop; for home-bred medicines are both more easy for the parson's purse, and more familiar for all men's bodies. So, where the apothecary useth either for loosing, rhubarb, or for binding, bolearmena, the parson useth damask or white roses for the one, and plantain, shepherd's-purse, knot-grass for the other, and that with better success. As for spices, he doth not only prefer home-bred things before them, but condemns them for vanities and so shuts them out of his family, esteeming that there is no spice comparable for herbs to rosemary, thyme, savory, mints; and for seeds to fennel and carraway-seeds. Accordingly, for salves, his wife seeks not the city, but prefers her garden and fields, before all outlandish gums.

A Priest to the Temple; or The Country Parson,
His Character and Rule of Holy Life
GEORGE HERBERT
(1593–1632)

Horse-radish – as a weed, I know of nothing quite so pertinacious and pernicious as this: I know of nothing but fire which will destroy its powers of vegetation … But, as a vegetable, it is a very fine thing.

The English Gardener
WILLIAM COBBETT
(1762–1835)

Then a sentimental passion
of a vegetable fashion
must excite your
languid spleen,
An attachment à la Plato
for a bashful young potato, or a
not-too-French French bean!

SIR WILLIAM SCHWENCK GILBERT
(1836–1911)

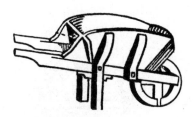

I came to love my rows, my beans, though so many more than I wanted. They attached me to the earth, and so I got strength like Antæus. But why should I raise them? Only Heaven knows.

HENRY DAVID THOREAU
(1817–1862)

It was one of the most bewitching sights in the world to observe a hill of beans thrusting aside the soil, or a row of early peas peeping forth sufficiently to trace a line of delicate green. Later in the season the humming-birds were attracted by the blossoms of a peculiar variety of bean; and they were a joy to me ... Multitudes of bees used to busy themselves in the yellow blossoms of the summer squashes.

The Old Manse
NATHANIEL HAWTHORNE
(1807–64)

Who would look dangerously up at planets that might safely look down at plants?

The Herball
JOHN GERARD
(1545–1612)

Unwelcome Visitors

SLUGS AND SNAILS HAVE BEEN in your garden before the time of Stonehenge; and no doubt, whatever you do, they'll still be there when your great, great grandchildren think they are the owners and masters of your garden. Rabbits may appear fluffy and cuddly in someone else's field; they are not so endearing if it is your carrot crop they have just destroyed.

The insect that infests turnips and many crops in the garden (destroying often whole fields while in their seedling leaves) is an animal that wants to be better known. The country people here call it the turnip-fly and black dolphin; but I know it to be one of the *coleoptera*; the *chrysomela oleracea, saltatoria, femoribus posficis crassissimis*. In very hot summers they abound to an amazing degree, and as you walk in a field or in a garden, make a pattering like rain, by jumping on the leaves of the turnips or cabbages.

The Natural History of Selborne
GILBERT WHITE
(1720–93)

Snail I was born, and snail shall end.
And what's a butterfly? At best,
He's but a caterpillar, drest:
And all thy race (a numerous seed)
Shall prove of caterpillar breed.

'Fable'
JOHN GAY
(1685–1732)

Mice are great enemies of beans, or, more properly, they love them too much, as the cannibal said of his fellow man.

The English Gardener
WILLIAM COBBETT
(1762–1835)

Neighbors' hens in your garden are an annoyance. Even if they did not scratch up the corn, and peck the strawberries, and eat the tomatoes, it is not pleasant to see them straddling about in their jerky, high-stepping, speculative manner, picking inquisitively here and there. It is of no use to tell the neighbor that his hens eat your tomatoes: it makes no impression on him, for the tomatoes are not his. The best way is to casually

remark to him that he has a fine lot of chickens, pretty well grown, and that you like spring chickens broiled. He will take them away at once.

My Summer in a Garden
CHARLES DUDLEY WARNER
(1829–1900)

The moles nested in my cellar, nibbling every third potato, and making a snug bed even there of some hair left after plastering and of brown paper; for even the wildest animals love comfort and warmth as well as man, and they survive the winter only because they are so careful to secure them.

HENRY DAVID THOREAU
(1817–62)

Mole hills in the garden are not helpful when you are trying to sell your house.

ESTATE AGENT
1999

She goes but softly, but she goeth sure,
She stumbles not as stronger creatures do;
Her journeys shorter, so she may endure
Better than they which do much further go.

She makes no noise, but stilly seizeth on
The flower or herb appointed for her food,
The which she quietly doth feed upon,
While others range and gare but find no good.

And though she doth but very softly go,
However 'tis not fast nor slow but sure;
And certainly they that do travel so,
The prize they do aim at, they do procure.

'Upon The Snail'
JOHN BUNYAN
(1628–88)

Weaving spiders, come not here;
Hence, you longlegged spinners, hence!
Beetles black approach not near;
Worm nor snail, do no offence.

WILLIAM SHAKESPEARE
(1564–1616)

The great pests of a garden are wasps, which destroy all the finer fruits just as they are coming into perfection. In 1781 we had none; in 1783 there were myriads; which would have devoured all the produce of my garden, had not we set the boys to take the nests, and caught thousands with hazel twigs tipped with bird-lime.

The Natural History of Selborne
GILBERT WHITE
(1720–93)

I scorn the doubts and cares that hurt
    The world and all its mockeries
My only care is now to squirt
    The ferns among my rockeries.

From 'A Garden Song'
GEORGE R. SIMMS
(1847–1922)

A cow is a very good animal in the field; but we turn her out of a garden.

SAMUEL JOHNSON.
(1709–84)

The other day I went to my garden to get a mess of peas. I had seen, the day before, that they were just ready to pick. How I had lined the ground, planted, hoed, bushed them! The bushes were very fine, – seven feet high, and of good wood. How I had delighted in the growing, the blowing, the podding! What a touching thought it was that they had all podded for me! When I went to pick them, I found the pods all split open, and the peas gone. The dear little birds, who are so fond of the strawberries, had eaten them all. Perhaps there were left as many as I planted: I did not count them. I made a rapid estimate of the

128

cost of the seed, the interest of the ground, the price of labor, the value of the bushes, the anxiety of weeks of watchfulness. I looked about me on the face of Nature. The wind blew from the south so soft and treacherous! A thrush sang in the woods so deceitfully! All Nature seemed fair. But who was to give me back my peas? The fowls of the air have peas; but what has man?

My Summer in a Garden
CHARLES DUDLEY WARNER
(1829–1900)

And it's all well and good saying let your garden be a sanctuary for wild life. I am dive bombed whenever I go to the tool shed where the swallows are nesting; the plums are covered in wasps; and a fat thrush is sitting in the fig tree.

Letter
SYLVIA BELL
(1932–)

When Morrice view his prostrate peas,
　　By raging whirlwinds spread,
He wrings his hands, and in amaze
　　He sadly shakes his his head.

'Is this the fruit of my fond toil,
　　My joy, my pride, my cheer!
Shall one tempestuous hour thus spoil
　　The labours of a year!

Ah! what avails, that day to day
　　I nursed the thriving crop,
And settled with my foot the clay,
　　And reared the social prop!'

Ah! Morris cease thy fruitless moan,
Nor at misfortunes spurn,
Misfortune's not thy lot alone;
    Each neighbour hath his turn.

Thy prostrate peas, which low recline,
    Beneath the frowns of fate,
May teach much wiser heads than thine
    Their own uncertain state.

'On a Fine Crop of Peas
Being Spoiled by a Storm'
HENRY JONES
(1721–70)

Ants, to destroy. Place an inverted garden-pot over the nest, and the ants will work into it. Remove the pot in a day or two by placing a spade underneath it; then plunge it, with its contents, into boiling water, and repeat the process if necessary.

Beeton's New Dictionary of Every-day Gardening
SAM BEETON
1862

The city mouse lives in a house; —
The garden mouse lives in a bower.

CHRISTINA GEORGINA ROSSETTI
(1830–94)

In the Middle Ages the monks in St. Bernard's ascetic community at Clairvaux excommunicated a vineyard which a less rigid monk had planted near, so that it bore nothing. In 1120 a bishop of Laon excommunicated the caterpillars in his diocese; and, the following year, St. Bernard excommunicated the flies in the Monastery of Foigny; and in 1510 the ecclesiastical court pronounced the dread sentence against the rats of Autun, Macon, and Lyons.

My Summer in a Garden
CHARLES DUDLEY WARNER
(1829–1900)

When black snails on the road you see
Then on the morrow, rain will be.

OLD SAYING

The butterfly, an idle thing,
Nor honey makes, nor yet can sing,
    As do the bee and bird;
Nor does it, like the prudent ant,
Lay up the grain for times of want,
    A wise and cautions hoard.

My youth is but a summer's day
Then like the bee and ant I'll lay
    A store of learning by;
And though from flower to flower I rove,
My stock of wisdom I'll improve
    Nor be a butterfly.

The Butterfly
JANE AND ANN TAYLOR
(1783–1824 and 1782–1866)

The neighbors' small children are also out of place in your garden, in strawberry and currant time. I hope I appreciate the value of children. We should soon come to nothing without them … But the problem is, what to do with them in a garden. For they are not good to eat, and there is a law against making away with them.

My Summer in a Garden
CHARLES DUDLEY WARNER
(1829–1900)

A testy old gardener said 'Why
Am I constantly plagued with greenfly?
Though I've squished and I've squirted
They're not even hurted!
What wilful refusal to die!'

P.J.M.

Of all the intolerable bores who visit us is the man who brings his own place with him, and who, whatever may be shown to him, at once institutes a comparison with his own, and begins to tell that 'mine are much better than that' – 'I can beat you on so and so,' and ignoring the thing before him tells us 'Ah, you should see my strawberries', 'my roses', 'my tomatoes' and so on all through – in short the man who does not 'shut his own gate behind him'.

The Amateur Gardener
JANE LOUDON
1847

Slugs and snails are perhaps the worst pests of a heavy soil, and there is no means of extirpating them. They can only be dealt with in detail by killing all that are encountered and by surrounding the plants for which they have particular fancy with soot or ashes. Not only is the voracity of slugs, though vegetarian, comparable with that of sharks and crocodiles when the difference of size is considered, but they have also a horrible epicurism of taste which will not be satisfied by an innocent meal off the leaves of vigorous and full-grown plants. They make for whatever is young and tender, and are happy when they can kill where they dine.

The Times, 16th March 1907

I like also little Heaps, in the Nature of Mole-hills ... to be set, some with Wilde Thyme; some with Pinks ... some with Violets; some with Strawberries ... And the like Low Flowers, being withal Sweet, and sightly.

FRANCIS BACON
(1561–1626)

There's a cat in the garden a-laying for a rat,
There's a boy with a catapult a-laying for the cat;
The cat's name is Susan, the boy's name is Jim,
And his father round the corner is a-laying
    for him.

ANON.

Brown and furry
Caterpillar in a hurry,
Take your walk
To the shady leaf, or stalk,
Or what not,
Which may be the chosen spot.
No toad spy you,
Hovering bird of prey pass by you;
Spin and die,
To live again a butterfly.

The Caterpillar
CHRISTINA GEORGINA ROSSETTI
(1830–94)

Friends and Neighbours

HOW WELCOME ARE THE swallows in the spring and the voice of the distant cuckoo; how unwelcome the magpie that pecks our milk and the mangy fox who strews the rubbish from our neighbour's bin on our lawn ... they have their human counterparts.

A certain swallow built for two years together on the handles of a pair of garden-shears, that were stuck up against the boards in an out-house, and therefore must have her nest spoiled whenever that implement was wanted.

The Natural History of Selborne
GILBERT WHITE
(1720–93)

I never stay anywhere, where there is a garden, without bringing back with me one or more shrubs, as a rememberance of a beautiful place or happy hour; and, when I plant them, I fasten to them a label, mentioning their old home, and thus I am reminded – now of a quaint low house covered with creepers, nestling among the hills of Wales – now of a magnificent castle in the north of Ireland – now of a great hall in Scotland – now of an old English abbey, where the flowers of today spring up among the ruins of a thousand years ago.

A Year in a Lancashire Garden
HENRY BRIGHT
1901

I send you, my dearest Emily ... the four white oenotheras, the blue pea, the Salpiglossis picta, the white Clarkia, a new lupine, the most beautiful that I have ever seen, but a clear lilac and clear white, and of far larger spikes of flowers (I enclose a flower), a new annual chrysanthemum (Cape marigold) with yellow outer leaves ... and two little packets of seeds from Madeira, sent me by a gentleman whom I

have never either seen or even heard of till now, but who, having been ordered there for his health, took my books with him, and found them of so much amusement to him that he sent me some seeds on his arrival by way of return, and we are likely to become great friends.

Private letter
MARY RUSSELL MITFORD
(1757–1855)

Good huswifes in sommer will save their own seedes, Against the next yeere, as occasion needes. One seede for another, to make an exchange, With fellowlie neigbourhood seemeth not strange.

A Year in a Lancashire Garden
HENRY BRIGHT
1901

You ask what is the use of butterflies; I reply, to adorn the world and delight the eyes of men: to brighten the countryside like so many golden jewels. To contemplate their exquisite beauty and variety is to experience the truest pleasure. To gaze inquiringly at such elegance of colour and form designed by the ingenuity of nature and painted by her artist's pencil is to acknowledge and adore the imprint of the art of God.

JOHN RAY
(1627–1705)

The old Sussex tortoise ... is become my property. I dug it out of its winter dormitory in March last, when it was enough awakened to express its resentments by hissing; and, packing it in a box with earth, carried it eighty miles in post-chaises. The rattle and hurry of the journey so perfectly roused it that, when I turned it out on a border, it walked twice down to the bottom of my garden; however, in the evening, the weather being cold, it buried itself in the loose mould, and continues still concealed.

When one reflects on the state of this strange being, it is a matter of wonder to find that Providence should bestow such a profusion of days, such a seeming waste of longevity, on a reptile that appears to relish it so little as to squander more than two-thirds of its existence in a joyless stupor, and be lost to all sensation for months together in the profoundest of slumbers.

The Natural History of Selborne
GILBERT WHITE
(1720–93)

143

Never, I could fancy, did autumn clothe in such magnificence the elms and birches; never, I should think, did the leafage on my walls blaze in such royal crimson. Was it for five minutes, or was it for an hour that I watched the yellow butterfly wafted as if by an insensible tremor of air amid the garden glintings? In every autumn there comes one such flawless day.

GEORGE GISSING
(1857–1903)

I've watched you now a full half-hour,
Self-poised upon that yellow flower;
And, little Butterfly! indeed!
I know not if you sleep or feed.
How motionless!—not frozen seas
More motionless; and then
What joy awaits you, when the breeze
Hath found you out among the trees,
And calls you forth again!

This plot of orchard ground is ours;
My trees they are, my sister's flowers;
Here rest your wings when they are weary,
Here lodge as in a sanctuary!
Come often to us, fear no wrong;
Sit near us on the bough!
We'll talk of sunshine and of song:
And summer days, when we were young;
Sweet childish days, that were as long
As twenty days are now.

'To a Butterfly'
WILLIAM WORDSWORTH
(1770–1850)

The caterpillar on the leaf
Repeats to thee thy mother's grief.
Kill not the moth, nor butterfly.
For the Last Judgement draweth nigh.

WILLIAM BLAKE
(1757–1827)

While I was writing this letter, a moist and warm afternoon, with the thermometer at 50, brought forth a troupe of shell-snails; and, at the same juncture, the tortoise heaved up the mould and put out its head; and the next morning came forth, as it were raised from the dead; and walked about till four in the afternoon.

The Natural History of Selborne
GILBERT WHITE
(1720–93)

What pleasure is there greater than to go round one's garden on a sunny day with a fellow-enthusiast, and to sing that cheering Litany which runs, in strophe and antistrophe, 'oh, wouldn't you like a bit of this?' – 'And I could send you a bulb of that'. Down delves the glad trowel into a clump, and it is halved – like mercy, blessing him that gives and him that takes … There are few greater pleasures in life than giving pleasure with a plant; or getting pleasure again with a plant. And certainly there is none more bland and blameless.

In A Yorkshire Garden
REGINALD JOHN FARRER
(1880–1920)

You, my own Emily, gave me my first plants of the potentilla, and very often as I look at them I think of you. You must send me some little seed in a letter, as a return for these plants, seeds of your own gathering and from your own garden, and it shall go hard but I will make them grow: any seed that you think pretty.

Private letter
MARY RUSSELL MITFORD
(1757–1855)

I would say generally that the love of flowers
and gardening is so universal amongst the
English peasantry that a country parson will
often find a better introduction to a cottager
through his garden than by any other means. And
though the love of flowers is so universal, and the
garden may be such a useful adjunct to the
cottage, yet there is a very great ignorance of the
right principles of gardening, and the parson may
be of great use to his poorer neighbours, not
only by teaching, but still more by showing them

better ways in his own garden. For the parsonage garden gate should be always open, and every parishioner welcomed; there need to be no fear of any undue advantage being taken of the free permission to enter – the one difficulty will be to induce them to come in. And the parson may do much to brighten the gardens of his parish, and so to increase the interest in them by giving plants from his own garden. I have for many years been a cultivator of hardy plants, and have been able to gather together a large number of species; and I was long ago taught, and have always held, that it is impossible to get or keep a large collection except by constant liberality in giving … and the parson who is liberal with his plants will find the increase not only in the pleasant intercourse with his neighbours, but also in the enlargement of his own garden, which thus spreads beyond his own fences into the gardens of the cottages.

In a Gloucestershire Garden
CANON ELLACOMBE
1895

But the nightingale, another of my airy creatures, breathes such sweet loud music out of her little instrumental throat, that it might make mankind to think miracles are not ceased. He that at midnight, when the very labourer sleeps securely, should hear, as I have very often, the clear airs, the sweet descant, the natural rising and falling, the doubling and redoubling of her voice, might well be lifted above earth, and say 'Lord, what music hast Thou provided for the saints in heaven, when Thou affordest bad men such music on earth.'

IZAAK WALTON
(1593–1683)

What is more cheerful, now, in the fall of the year, than an open-wood-fire? Do you hear those little chirps and twitters coming out of that piece of apple-wood? Those are the ghosts of the robins and blue-birds that sang upon the bough when it was in blossom last Spring. In Summer whole flocks of them come fluttering about the fruit-trees under the window: so I have singing birds all the year round.

Miss Mehitabel's Son
THOMAS BAILEY ALDRICH
(1836–1907)

My banks they are furnish'd with bees
    Whose murmur invites one to sleep
My grottoes are shaded wtih trees
    And my hills are white over with sheep.

WILLIAM SHENSTONE
(1714–63)

Buzzing, buzzing, buzzing, my golden-belted
    bees:
My little son was seven years old – the mint-
    flower touched his knees;
Yellow were his curly locks;
Yellow were his stocking-clocks;
His plaything of a sword had a diamond in its hilt;
Where the garden beds lay sunny,
And the bees were making honey,
'For God and the King—to arms! to arms!' the
    day long would he lilt.

Flitting, flitting over the thyme, my bees with
    yellow band ...

from 'The Bees of Myddelton Manor'
MAY PROBYN
(17th Century)

If bees stay at home, rain will come soon;
if they fly away, fine will be the day.

COUNTRY LORE

Down a winding glade with leaflets wall'd,
With an odorous dewy dark imbued;
Rose, and maple, and hazel call'd
Me into the shadowy solitude;
Wild blue germander eyes enthrall'd
Made me free of the balmy bowers,
Where a wonderful garden-party of flowers,
Laughing sisterhood under the trees,
Dancing merrily, play'd with the bees;

The Secret of the Nightingale
RODEN BERKELEY WRIOTHESLEY NOEL
(1834—94)

Birds should be encouraged rather than destroyed in a garden, provided that the fruits are protected by nets, and cherry trees. They pick up not only caterpillars but the seeds of weeds.

The Garden Notebook
CAROLINE HAMILTON
(1827—46)

God, and The Virtues of Gardening

*T*HERE IS NO BETTER WAY OF *disposing of daily cares and vexations than leaning on a spade in the garden and forgetting about all that is beyond. Enter a gentle paradise of your own.*

A garden is a lovesome thing, God wot!
    Rose plot,
    Fringed pool,
Fern'd grot –
    The veriest school
    Of peace; and yet the fool
Contends that God is not –
Not God! in gardens! when the eve is cool?
    Nay, but I have a sign;
    'Tis very sure God walks in mine.

'My Garden'
THOMAS EDWARD BROWN
(1830–97)

A garden that one makes oneself becomes associated with one's personal history and that of one's friends, interwoven with one's tastes, preferences and character, and constitutes a sort of unwritten, but withal manifest, autobiography. Show me your garden, provided it be your own, and I will tell you what you are like.

The Garden that I love
ALFRED AUSTIN
(1835–1913)

Die when I may, I want it said of me by those who know me best, that I always plucked a thistle and planted a flower where I thought a flower would grow.

ABRAHAM LINCOLN
(1809–65)

I am heartily in sympathy with the feeling described in these words in a friend's letter

'I think there are few things so interesting as to see in what way a person, whose perceptions you think fine and worthy of study, will give them expression in a garden.'

Wood and Garden
GERTRUDE JEKYLL
(1843–1932)

After this, he (the Interpreter) led them into his Garden where was great Variety of Flowers: And he said, Do you see all these? So Christian said, Yes. Then said he again, Behold the Flowers are divers in Stature, in Quality, and Colour, Smell, and Virtue; and some are better than some: where the Gardener hath set them, there they stand, and quarrel not one with another.

When the Interpreter had done, he takes them out into his Garden again, and had them to a Tree, whose inside was all rotten and gone, and yet it grew and had leaves. Then said Mercy, What means this? This Tree, said he, whose Outside is fair and whose Inside is rotten, it is, to which may be compared, that are in the Garden of God: Who with their Mouths speak high in Behalf of God, but in deed will do nothing for him; whose Leaves are fair, but their Hearts good for nothing but to be Tinder for the Devil's Tinder-Box.

The Pilgrim's Progress
JOHN BUNYAN
(1628–88)

And the Lord God planted a garden eastward in
  Eden; and there he put the man whom he
  had formed.
And out of the ground made the Lord God to
  grow every tree that is pleasant to the sight,
  and good for food; the tree of life also in the
  midst of the garden, and the tree of knowledge of good and evil.
And a river went out of Eden to water the
  garden; and from thence it was parted, and
  became into four heads.

Genesis

The story of mankind began in a
garden and ended in Revelations.

OSCAR WILDE
(1854–1900)

Adam was, and dwelled towards the East in Syria and Arabia, when hee was created: but after hee had sinned, then it was no more so delightful and pleasant.

Even so in our time hath God cursed likewise fruitful lands, and hath caused them to bee barren and unfruitful by reason of our sins: for where God gives not His blessing, there grows nothing that is good and profitable; but where He blesseth, there all things grow plentifully, and are fruitful.

Colloquia [Table Talk]
MARTIN LUTHER
(1483–1546)

What do thy noontide walks avail,
To clear the leaf, and pick the snail,
Then wantonly to death decree
An insect usefuller than thee?
Thou and the worm are brother-kind,
As low, as earthy, and as blind.

'The Dying Man in His Garden'
G. SEWELL

What would the world be, once bereft
Of wet and of wildness? Let them be left,
O Let them be left, wildness and wet:
Long live the weeds and the wilderness yet.

from *Inversnaid*
GERARD MANLEY HOPKINS
(1844–89)

The principal value of a private garden is not understood. It is not to give the possessor vegetables and fruit (that can be better and cheaper done by the market-gardeners), but to teach him patience and philosophy, and the higher virtues, — hope deferred, and expectations blighted, leading directly to resignation and sometimes to alienation. The garden thus becomes an agent, a test of character, as it was in the beginning.

My Summer in a Garden
CHARLES DUDLEY WARNER
(1829–1900)

'Tis the voice of the Sluggard; I heard him
   complain,
'You have waked me too soon; I must
    slumber again';
  As the door on its hinges, so he on his bed
Turns his sides, and his shoulders, and his
   heavy head.

I pass'd by his garden, and saw the wild brier,
The thorn and the thistle, grow broader
    and higher;
The clothes that hang on him are turning to
   rags;
And his money still wastes till he starves
   or he begs.

From 'The Sluggard'
ISAAC WATTS
(1674–1748)

But for him who feareth the majesty of his
    Lord shall be two gardens:
With trees branched over:
And therein two flowing wells
And therein of every fruit two kinds:
Reclining on couches with linings of brocade
    and the fruit of the gardens to their hand:
Therein the shy-eyed maidens neither man
    nor Jinn hath touched before:
Like rubies and pearls:
Shall the reward of good be aught but good?

Speeches of Mohammad
translated by STANLEY LANE POOLE
(1854–1931)

Like other boys in the country, I had my patch
of ground, to which, in the spring-time, I
intrusted the seed furnished me, with a confident

trust in their resurrection and glorification in the better world of summer.

But I soon found that my lines had fallen in a place where a vegetable growth had to run the gauntlet of as many foes and trials as a Christian pilgrim. Flowers would not blow; daffodils perished like criminals in their condemned cups, without their petals ever seeing daylight; roses were disfigured with monstrous protrusions ... lettuces and cabbages would not head; radishes knotted themselves until they looked like centenarian's fingers; and on every stem, on every leaf; and at the root of everything that grew, was a professional specialist in the shape of a gnat, caterpillar, aphis, or other expert, whose business it was to ... help murder the whole attempt at vegetation. Such experiences must influence a child born to them. A sandy soil, where nothing flourishes but weeds and evil beasts of small dimensions, must breed different qualities in its human offspring from one of those fat and fertile spots.

The Poet at the Breakfast Table
OLIVER WENDELL HOLMES
(1809–94)

You must know, Sir, that I look upon the pleasure which we take in a Garden, as one of the most innocent delights in human Life. A Garden was the habitation of our first parents before the fall. It is naturally apt to fill the mind with calmness and tranquillity, and to lay all its turbulent passions at rest. It gives us a great insight into the contrivance and wisdom of providence, and suggests innumerable subjects for meditation. I cannot but think the very complacency and satisfaction which a man takes in these works of Nature to be a laudable if not a virtuous habit of mind.

The Spectator, 6th Sept 1712
JOSEPH ADDISON
(1672–1719)

I do not envy the owners of very large gardens. The garden should fit its master or his tastes, just as his clothes do; it should be neither too large nor too small, but just comfortable.

Wood and Garden
GERTRUDE JEKYLL
(1843–1932)

I know a lady, a member of the church, and a very good sort of woman, considering the subject condition of that class, who says that the weeds work on her to that extent, that, in going through her garden, she has the greatest difficulty in keeping the ten commandments in anything like an unfractured condition. I asked her which one, but she said, all of them: one felt like breaking the whole lot.

My Summer in the Garden
CHARLES DUDLEY WARNER
(1829–1900)

The prayer of the farmer kneeling in his field to weed it; the prayer of the rower, kneeling with the stroke of his oar, are true prayers heard throughout nature.

RALPH WALDO EMERSON
(1803–82)

Gentlewomen if the ground be not too wet, may doe themselves much good by Kneeling upon a Cushion and weeding. And thus both sexes might divert themselves from Idlenesse and evill Company.

Art of Simpling
WILLIAM COLES
1656

We will endeavour to shew how the aire and genious of Gardens operate upon human spirits towards virtue and sancitie, I meane in a remote, preparatory and instrumentall working. How Caves, Grotts, Mounts, and irregular ornaments of Gardens do contribute to contemplative and philosophicall

Enthusiasms ... for these expedients do influence the soule and spirits of man, and prepare them for converse with good Angells; besides which, they contribute to the lesse abstracted pleasures, phylosophy naturall and longevitie.

JOHN EVELYN to Sir Thomas Browne
1657

The kiss of the sun for pardon,
  The song of the birds for mirth,
One is nearer God's Heart in a garden
  Than anywhere else on earth.

God's Garden
DOROTHY FRANCIS GURNEY
(1858–1932)

Love in The Garden

*I*N THE DUSK OF A SUMMER evening as the musk of the roses envelopes the still of the garden and all the business of the world fades, who does not long for a hand to hold and a heart to clasp to one's own?

And now what monarch would not gardener be,
My fair Amanda's stately gait to see;
How her feet tempt! How soft and light she
    treads,
Fearing to wake the flowers from their beds!
Yet from their sweet green pillows everywhere,
They start and gaze about to see my fair.

From 'To Amanda Walking in the Garden'
NICHOLAS HOOKES
(1628–1712)

And yet, in accord with theories she believed
right, she wanted to make herself in love
with him. By moonlight in the garden she recited
all the passionate rhymes she knew by heart, and,
sighing, sang to him many melancholy adagios;
but she found herself as calm after as before, and
Charles seemed no more amorous and no more
moved.

Madame Bovary
GUSTAVE FLAUBERT
(1821–80)

I passed by a garden, a little Dutch garden,
  Where useful and pretty things grew, –
Heart's-ease and tomatoes, and pinks and
    potatoes,
  And lilies and onions and rue.

I saw in that garden, that little Dutch garden,
  A chubby Dutch man with a spade,
And a rosy Dutch frau with a shoe like a scow,
  And a flaxen haired little Dutch maid.

There grew in that garden, that little Dutch
    garden,
  Blue flag flowers lovely and tall,
And early blush roses, and little pink posies,
  But Gretchen was fairer than all.

My heart 's in that garden, that little Dutch
  garden, –
  It tumbled right in as I passed,
Mid wildering mazes of spinach and daisies,
And Gretchen is holding it fast.

> 'A Little Dutch Garden'
> HATTIE WHITNEY
> 1900

'Tis down in yonder garden green
  Love, where we used to walk,
The finest flower that ere was seen
  Is withered to the stalk.

> BALLAD

There is a garden in her face
    Where roses and white lilies grow;
A heavenly paradise is that place,
    Wherein all pleasant fruits do flow;
There cherries grow that none may buy,
'Till 'Cherry-Ripe' themselves do cry.

Those cherries fairly do enclose
    Of orient pearl a double row,
Which when her lovely laughter shows,
    They look like rosebuds fill'd with snow;
Yet them nor peer nor prince may buy,
'Till 'Cherry-Ripe' themselves do cry.

Her eyes like angels watch them still,
  Her brows like bended bows do stand,
Threat'ning with piercing frowns to kill
  All that approach with eye or hand
These sacred cherries to come nigh,
'Till 'Cherry-Ripe' themselves do cry.

'Cherry-Ripe'
THOMAS CAMPION
(1567–1620)

My lady's presence make the roses red,
Because to see her lips they blush for shame:
The lilies' leaves, for envy, pale became,
And her white hands in them this envy bred.

From 'Of His Mistress,
upon Occasion of her Walking in a Garden'
HENRY CONSTABLE
(1526–1613)

Come into the garden, Maud,
　For the black bat, Night, has flown,
Come into the garden, Maud,
　I am here at the gate alone;
And the woodbine spices are wafted abroad,
　And the musk of the roses blown.

There has fallen a splendid tear
　From the passion-flower at the gate.
She is coming, my dove, my dear;
　She is coming, my life, my fate;

The red rose cries, 'She is near, she is near;'
 And the white rose weeps, 'She is late;'
The larkspur listens, 'I hear, I hear;'
 And the lily whispers, 'I wait.'

She is coming, my own, my sweet;
 Were it ever so airy a tread,
My heart would hear her and beat,
 Were it earth in an earthy bed;
My dust would hear her and beat,
 Had I lain for a century dead;
Would start and tremble under her feet,
 And blossom in purple and red.

From 'Maud'
ALFRED LORD TENNYSON
(1809–92)

There may have been a time when my heart tempted me elsewhere; but now my greatest delight is to sit on a summer's evening in my garden with a glass of port and the love of my life; an hour's cigar.

SEPTIMUS SANDS
(1854–1900)

Did you not hear My Lady
Go down the garden singing
Blackbird and thrush were silent
To hear the alleys ringing …

Oh saw you not My Lady
Out in the garden there
Shaming the rose and lily
For she is twice as fair.
Though I am nothing to her
Though she must rarely look at me
And though I could never woo her
I love her till I die.

Surely you heard My Lady
Go down the garden singing
Silencing all the songbirds
And setting the alleys ringing …
But surely you see My Lady
Out in the garden there
Rivalling the glittering sunshine
With a glory of golden hair.

NICOLA FRANCESCO HAYM
1711

Soon it would be spring, summer, going with her mother to Gorbiki. Gorny would come for his furlough, would walk about the garden with her and make love to her. Gruzdev would come too. He would play croquet and skittles with her, and would tell her wonderful things. She had a passionate longing for the garden, the darkness, the pure sky, the stars. Again her shoulders shook with laughter, and it seemed to her that there was a scent of wormwood in the room and that a twig was tapping at the window.

After The Theatre
ANTON PAVLOVICH CHEKHOV
(1860–1904)

Have you ever been in love, me boys, Oh! have
    you felt the pain?
I'd rather be in jail, I would, than be in love
    again.
Tho' the girl I love is beautiful, and I'd have
    you all to know
That I met her in the garden where the
    praties [potatoes] grow.

TRADITIONAL IRISH SONG

Coming to kiss her lips (such grace I found,),
Meseem'd, I smelt a garden of sweet flowers.

EDMUND SPENSER
(1552?–99)

I suppose that when I saw Dora in the garden
and pretended not to see her, and rode past
the house pretending to be anxiously looking for
it, I committed two small fooleries which other
young gentlemen in my circumstances might
have committed – because they came so very
natural to me. But oh! when I did find the house,
and did dismount at the garden gate, and drag

178

those stony-hearted boots across the lawn to Dora sitting on a garden-seat under a lilac-tree, what a spectacle she was, upon that beautiful morning, among the butterflies, in a white chip bonnet and a dress of celestial blue! ... To see her lay the flowers against her little dimpled chin, was to lose all presence of mind and power of language in a feeble ecstasy. I wonder I didn't say, 'Kill me, if you have a heart, Miss Mills. Let me die here!'

David Copperfield
CHARLES DICKENS
(1812–70)

Fruit and The Orchard

*W*HAT A PALETTE OF *colour and flavours the fruit of our garden can offer us. Think of the first strawberry of June, of plum pies, of rhubarb crumble, of gooseberry fool, and all the jams and jellies we can feast upon.*

Lo! sweeten'd with the summer light,
The full juiced apple, waxing over-mellow,
Drops in a silent autumn night.

ALFRED, LORD TENNYSON
(1809–92)

You can count the number of apples on one tree, but you can never count the number of trees in one apple.

OLD PROVERB

If the caterpillar has begun its ravages, the ground beneath the currant bush should be sprinkled with new lime, and a double barrelled gun fired two or three times under it to shake the caterpillars down into it.

New Dictionary of Every-Day Gardening
SAM BEATON
1862

What can your eye desire to see, your cares to heare, your mouth to taste, or your nose to smell, that is not to be had in an orchard?

A New Orchard and Garden
WILLIAM LAWSON
1618

The red red'ning apple ripens here to gold,
Here the blue fig with lucious juice o'erflows,
With deeper red the full pomegranate glows,
The branch here bends beneath the weighty
	pear,
And verdant olives flourish round the year.
The balmy spirit western gale
Eternal breeze on fruits untaught to fail:
Each dropping pear a following pear supplies
On apples, apples, figs on figs arise.

from Homer's *Odyssey*, Book Vii
ALEXANDER POPE
(1688–1744)

182

Good is an Orchard, the Saint saith,
To meditate on life and death,
With a cool well, a hive of bees,
A hermit's grot below the trees.

Good is an Orchard; very good,
Though one should wear no monkish hood
Right good, when Spring awakes her flute,
And good in yellowing time of fruit.

Very good in the grass to lie
And see the network 'gainst the sky,
A living lace of blue and green,
And boughs that let the gold between.

Prayer and praise in a country home,
Honey and fruit: a man might come,
Fed on such meats, to walk abroad,
And in his Orchard talk with God.

KATHERINE TYNAN HINKSON
(1861–1931)

Vineyards, orchards, gardens and such enclos-
ed plots are the flowers, starres and paradises
of the earth… The World is a great Library, and
Fruit-trees are some of the Bookes wherein we
may read and see plainly the Attributes of God his
Power, Wisdome, Goodnesse, etc.

A Treatise of Fruit Trees Together with
The Sprituall Use of an Orchard
RALPH AUSTEN
1653

Now that glass is so cheap there
seems but little reason for growing
grapes out of doors.

The Tree Planter, Propagator and Pruner
SAMUEL WOOD
1894

184

PROVERB FOR APPLES, PEARS, HAWTHORNS, OAKES:

Sett [plant] them at All-Hallow-tide, and
    command them to grow,
Sett them at Candlemas and entreat them to
    grow.

OLD PROVERB

THE GARDEN AT 5 CHEYNE ROAD, CHELSEA

Behind we have a garden (so called in the language of flattery) in the worst of order, but boasting of two vines which produce two bunches of grapes in the season which 'might be eaten', and a walnut tree from which I gathered almost sixpence worth of Walnuts.

JANE CARLYLE
(1801–66)

Here we see that, even among berries, there are degrees of breeding. The currant is well enough, clear as truth, and excellent in colour; but I ask you to notice how far it is from the exclusive hauteur of the aristocratic strawberry and the native refinement of the quietly elegant raspberry.

My Summer in the Garden
CHARLES DUDLEY WARNER
(1829–1900)

Preserving strawberries from the birds and slugs. As to the first of these, the woodpigeons, the common pigeons … the thrushes and even some of the small birds, invade the strawberry clumps, and, if unresisted destroy a greater part of the fruit … nothing is a protection but a net … the slug is a still more bitter enemy; and in some seasons ... more than half the fruit is consumed by these nasty and mischievous reptiles. Remedy: see that there are no slugs about the stems of the leaves, and then make a little circle of hot lime, at half a foot or so at the extremity of the leaves of the clumps. No slug will enter that magic circle.

The English Gardener
WILLIAM COBBETT
(1762–1835)

The great men among the ancients under-stood very well how to reconcile manual labour with affairs of state, and thought it no lessening to their dignity to make the one the recreation to the other ... as I remember, Cyrus thought gardening so little beneath the dignity and grandeur of a throne, that he showed Xenophon a large field of fruit trees all of his own planting.

JOHN LOCKE
(1632–1704)

Swift had an odd humour of making extempore proverbs. Observing that a gentleman, in whose garden he walked with some friends, seemed to have no intention to request them to eat any of the fruit, Swift observed, It was a saying of his dear grandmother

> Always pull a peach
> When it is within your reach

and helping himself accordingly, his example was followed by the whole company.

Memoir of Jonathan Swift
SIR WALTER SCOTT
(1771–1832)

> He who plants pears,
> Plants for his heirs.

SAYING

And o'er the gardens, grown somewhat
    out-worn,
The bees go hurrying to fill up their store;
The apple-boughs bend over more and more;
With peach and apricot the garden wall,
Is odorous and the pears begin to fall
From off the high tree with each
    freshening breeze.

WILLIAM MORRIS
(1834–96)

My mind has been turned to the subject of fruit and shade trees in a garden. There are those who say that trees shade the garden too much, and interfere with the growth of the vegetables. There may be something in this: but when I go down the potato rows, the rays of the sun glancing upon my shining blade, the sweat pouring from my face, I should be grateful for shade. What is a garden for? The pleasure of man. I should take much more pleasure in a shady garden. Am I to be sacrificed, broiled, roasted, for the sake of the increased vigor of a few vegetables?

My Summer in a Garden
CHARLES DUDLEY WARNER
(1829–1900)

The nights were frosty, the mornings and evenings were misty, but at mid-day all was sunny and bright, and it was one mid-day that both of us being on the line near Heathbridge, and knowing that they were gathering apples at the farm, we resolved to spend the men's dinner-hour in going over there. We found the great clothes-baskets full of apples, scenting the house, and stopping up the way; and an universal air of

merry contentment with this the final produce of
the year. The yellow leaves hung on the trees
ready to flutter down at the slightest puff of air;
the great bushes of Michaelmas daisies in the
kitchen-garden were making their last show of
flowers. We must needs taste the fruit off the
different trees, and pass our judgment as to their
flavour; and we went away with our pockets
stuffed with those that we liked best.

Cousin Phillis
ELIZABETH GASKELL
(1810–65)

Go, little book, and wish to all
Flowers in the garden, meat in the hall,
A bin of wine, a spice of wit,
A house with lawns enclosing it,
A living river by the door,
A nightingale in the sycamore!

A Child's Garden of Verses and Underwoods
ROBERT LOUIS STEVENSON
(1850– 94)